5-MINUTE BASKETBALL STORIES

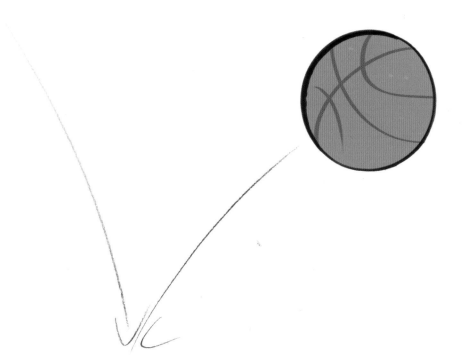

5-MINUTE BASKETBALL STORIES

Sarah Howden

Illustrations by Nick Craine

Collins

HarperCollins Publishers Ltd
Bay Adelaide Centre, East Tower
22 Adelaide Street West, 41st Floor
Toronto, Ontario, Canada
M5H 4E3

www.harpercollins.ca

Library and Archives Canada Cataloguing in Publication
information is available upon request.

Lettering design on pages 1, 15, 29, 43, 57, 71, 85, 99, 113, 127, 141, and 155 by Lola Landekic

ISBN 978-1-44345-672-2

Printed and bound in China
RRD/SC 9 8 7 6 5 4 3 2 1

Contents

STEPH CURRY
and the
COMEBACK

Finally, Steph Curry is back where he belongs: playing with the Golden State Warriors.

It'll be his first game since spraining his knee two weeks earlier. For Steph, those two weeks felt like forever.

It felt long for fans too. The team is good without him, sure, but he makes it great—with his agility, his quick thinking, his teamwork. Oh, and the points. He scores lots and lots of points.

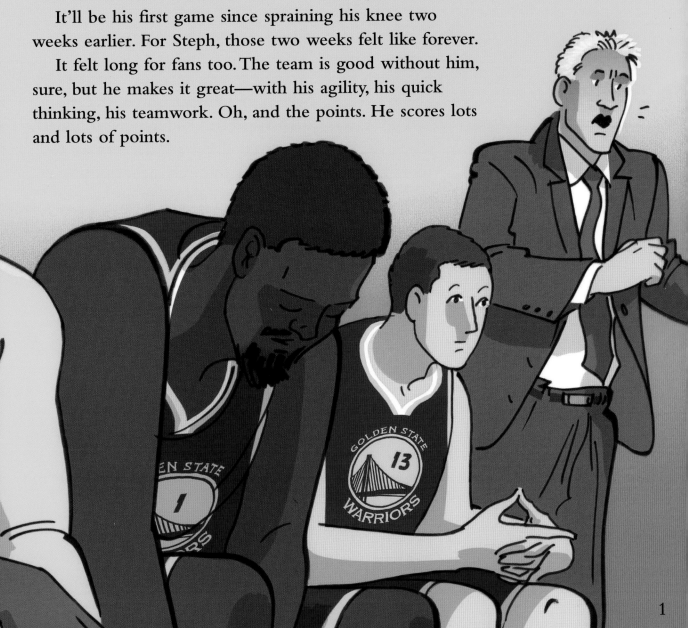

Now here he is, at Game 4 of the 2016 Western Conference semifinals. He's excited but a little nervous too. He knows you only need to miss a few games to get rusty.

Still, he's relieved when he steps out onto the court. He's in his element. Steph is home.

But soon he realizes something's not quite right.

He's making some baskets, but he's missing a few too. As the game goes on, it's more of the same. He's doing okay, but he feels out of step. He isn't quite back, and he knows it.

By the fourth quarter, he's getting into the flow, and he makes his first three-pointer. But it isn't enough. With the score tied and only a few seconds left, Steph fires a last shot at the basket . . . and misses. The game's going into overtime.

Steph can feel it: all those Warriors fans wondering, *Is he up to this?* And worse yet, the doubters. All the people saying, *I told you Curry isn't that good a player. I told you he doesn't deserve to be MVP.*

There have always been doubters, ever since he was a kid. Steph was small for his age, baby-faced, quiet. People would look at him and think, *He's not a threat.*

But what they couldn't see was how tough he was, how fast, how smart. And how the harder things got for him, the fiercer he would become.

He remembers the first time he let that fierceness out on the court. He was thirteen, playing for a tiny middle school in Toronto, Ontario. His team was on a winning streak.

But this one game, they were up against another top team who made it their mission to take Steph down. They blocked him at every turn, pushed him around.

Steph's team was behind by six points with about a minute left when the coach called a time-out. "Got any ideas?" he asked.

A switch inside Steph flipped. He spoke up. "Give me the ball. Give me the ball and we can win this."

When Steph got back out there, he found a new fire inside of himself. The other team tried to get in his way like before, but this time he was faster. Bolder. More determined.

First, Steph got one three-pointer. Then another. Just like that, he'd tied the game. In the end, his team won by six. It was clear: He might look small, but he was unstoppable.

A lot has changed now that he's an NBA champion, MVP, and all-star player. But facing overtime against the Blazers, Steph has that same look in his eyes: *Give me the ball and I can win this.*

The clock starts for the
overtime period, and it's
like Steph is in overdrive.
He's making shot after shot.

First two points, then a three-pointer, then another two-pointer . . .

The other team is scoring too, but Steph's on a roll. Another two points, then another three. He might have started out slow, but now he's at superspeed.

Blazers fans don't know what to think. Even the team's owner looks stunned.

Steph just outplays them. There's no way they can beat him. The Blazers are a good team, but he leaves them in the dust.

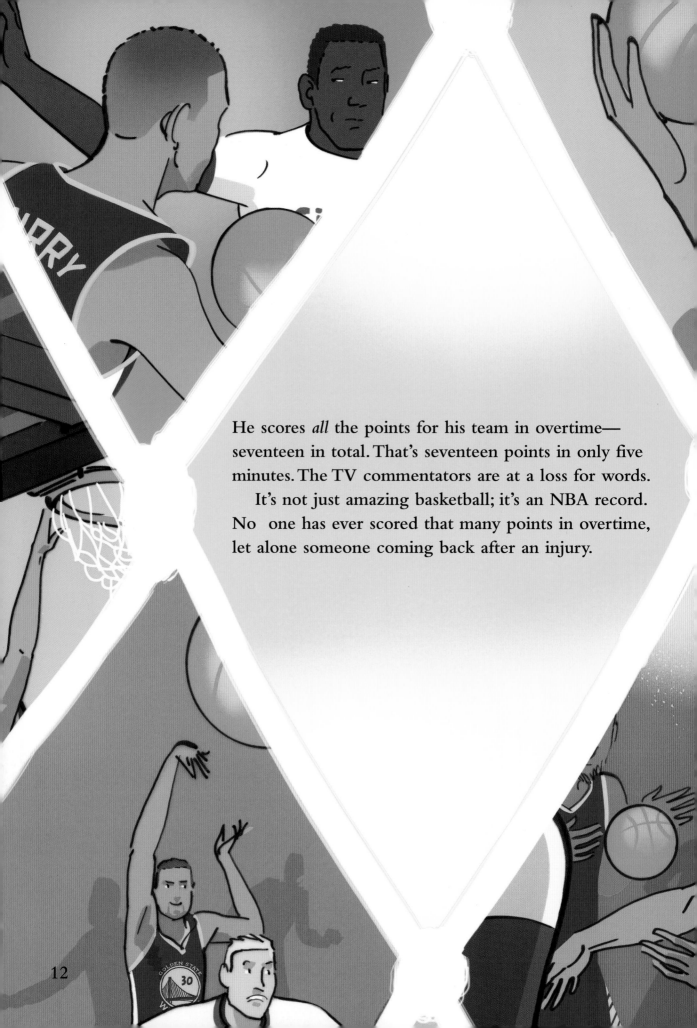

He scores *all* the points for his team in overtime—seventeen in total. That's seventeen points in only five minutes. The TV commentators are at a loss for words.

It's not just amazing basketball; it's an NBA record. No one has ever scored that many points in overtime, let alone someone coming back after an injury.

Warriors fans everywhere are cheering their hearts out, and Steph is grinning from ear to ear.

"I'm back," he says to the crowd—and no one, not even the doubters, can disagree with that.

BECOMING THE DREAM TEAM

The Dream Team. You've probably heard of them.
Greatest basketball team there ever was and probably
ever will be.

Michael Jordan. Magic Johnson. Larry Bird.
Patrick Ewing. John Stockton. And the list goes
on. Any one of those guys made a game
worth watching. And here were
twelve, all on the same team.

They came together in 1992 for the Summer Olympics in
Barcelona, Spain, and when they took their places in the
final showdown for Olympic gold, no one was surprised.
They hadn't lost a single game along the way.

   But if anyone had been sitting in the stands a few
weeks earlier in California, watching a practice scrimmage,
they would have seen something pretty unbelievable:
The Dream Team was looking weak.

Charles Barkley was getting dunked on. Larry Bird was missing baskets. Magic seemed out of step.

And the guys who were showing them up? A group of college kids called the Select Team. Excellent players, for sure, but younger and less experienced. What the Select Team did have, though, was their connection as a team and their drive to win.

During the short twenty-minute game, college player Allan Houston scored multiple three-pointers against the Dream Team. Ten in all. One of his teammates, Bobby Hurley, cut through their defense again and again, slicing a path right to the basket. And Chris Webber got a glorious slam dunk right over his heroes.

Meanwhile, the Dream Team was looking sloppy. Even though separately they were stars, together no one knew what role each player was meant to fill. So they just kept passing the ball back and forth. No one was playing their best, and they weren't scoring much either.

They were missing that spark, that momentum. Worse yet, they'd expected to win. And so the unthinkable happened: They lost.

It was a huge shock. Weren't they supposed to be the best of the best? Maybe these college guys should be in the Olympics instead . . .

The Dream Team's coach, Chuck Daly, wanted them to remember that moment. His message was clear. They might be superstars, but that didn't mean they couldn't lose. No matter how great they were, they would still need to work to win. And they'd need to work together.

After the game, he took them through some cooperative drills to get them thinking as a team. They had played against each other for so long, it was hard for them to realize they were all on the same side now. And that there was room for each of them to show their skills.

The coach promised them a rematch the next day, and the Dream Team could barely sleep that night. Now they had something to prove.

That next game couldn't have been more different. Michael Jordan owned the court. John Stockton stole the ball and passed it before the other team even knew it was gone. Bird scored some solid baskets. Magic was in the zone, moving the ball around at lightning speed.

The Selects were stunned. It was like
a completely different team, and they
couldn't get the ball past the center line.

By the end of the scrimmage, the Dream Team had beaten the Selects by more than a hundred points. Instead of expecting the win, this time, they had earned it.

They never forgot the lesson they'd learned thanks to the Selects. From then on, every game they played, they played their hardest. And they played as a team—looking out for each other, trusting each other, and giving each player the chance to shine.

After that, they really were the best in the world, no contest. At the Olympics, the Dream Team won all their games by an average of 43.8 points.

When it came time for the gold medal match against Croatia, everyone knew who was going to win. And this time there were no surprises—the Dream Team came through.

So many future Hall-of-Famers on the court together, wowing the crowd and bringing home the gold for their country. Not only were they the best in the world, together they were unbeatable.

GREATEST of ALL TIME

It's 1998, Game 6 of the NBA Finals, and you've got a lot on the line. This could be your last game with the Chicago Bulls, the team you've played with your entire NBA career.

It might even be the last time you'll ever play in the NBA.

But right now, the game could go either way.
If the Utah Jazz win, you'll need to play a
seventh game. But if your team wins tonight,
the Bulls take the championship. It would be a
great way to go out.

Everyone can feel it. The crowd is roaring.

There's only a minute left on the clock, and your team has called a time-out.

Everyone's tired. It has been a hard-fought game, and the score is close.

You're asking yourself, *Can we still win this?*

You're older now than you used to be—you can't jump quite as high or run quite as fast—but you're still the best. You know every inch of the court, and you know how to spot an opening. Any opening.

You think back to some tough moments. Moments that made you proud.

Game 5 of last season's NBA Finals: You were so sick, you hadn't slept, and your head was swimming. Weak and drained, you could barely sit up.

But once the game started, you got out there, and you played hard. Sweating buckets, you focused and gave everything you had. In the last twenty-eight seconds, you scored a three-pointer to win the championship.

And a few years before that, you were playing the Cleveland Cavaliers in the first round of the playoffs. The Bulls were down by one, and the crowd was celebrating as if your team had already lost. They thought the game was over.

With only three seconds left, you turned things around.

You got the ball, launched yourself into the air,
hung around there for what felt like a minute, took
a shot . . . and made the basket. The Bulls won.
People still talk about that play.

This game means a lot. Your team is counting on you. But you still have what you always had: your heart, your determination. And your belief in yourself.

You can shut out the crowd and just play. Play for the love of it. And play to win.

The time-out is over. You wipe your face with a towel and get back on the court.

First, you've got your free throws.
You step to the line, take a breath.
One: *swish.* Two: *swish.*
The score is tied.

But with forty seconds left,
the Jazz get the ball and sink a
three-pointer. The crowd, mostly
Utah fans, is going wild, but you
don't care.

You get the ball back, move in for a layup . . . and make the basket. Now the Bulls are behind by a single point.

The Jazz have the ball, and they're going to do all they can to keep it. But you're not going to let them.

You duck back, and the other team loses you, just for a split second. Like magic, you've faded into the background.

So Karl Malone doesn't see it coming when you reach around and steal the ball from him. You make it look easy.

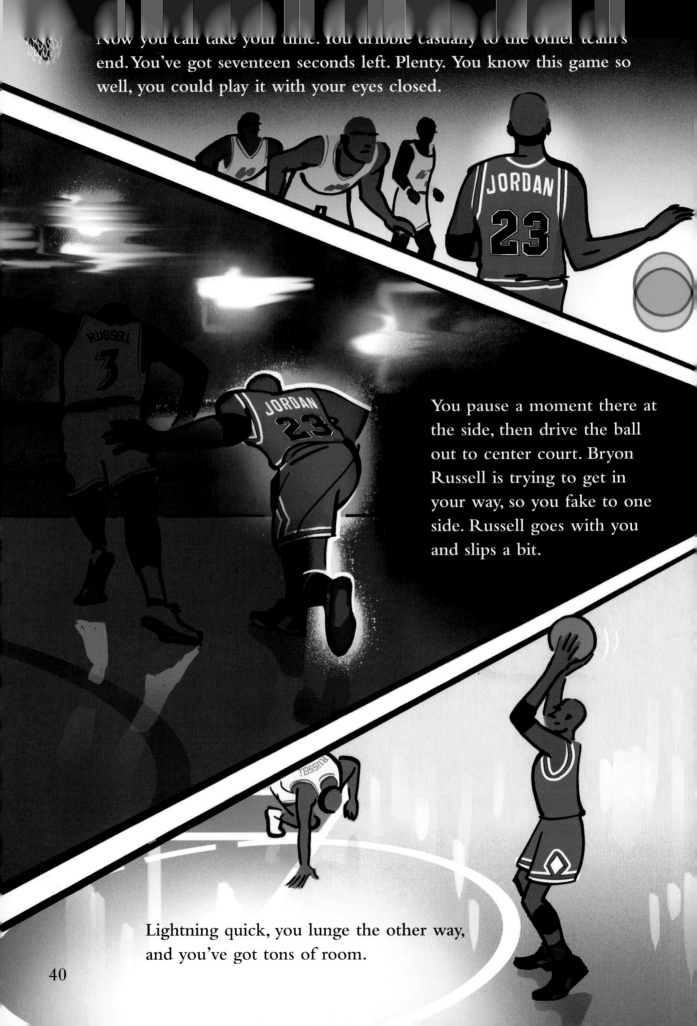

Now you can take your time. You dribble casually to the other team's end. You've got seventeen seconds left. Plenty. You know this game so well, you could play it with your eyes closed.

You pause a moment there at the side, then drive the ball out to center court. Bryon Russell is trying to get in your way, so you fake to one side. Russell goes with you and slips a bit.

Lightning quick, you lunge the other way, and you've got tons of room.

And so you do what you've always done, what feels so natural, and time stands still.

You jump, line up the shot, throw . . . and make a perfect basket.

The crowd is on its feet. Your mom, sitting courtside, has tears streaming down her face. The other team has five seconds left, but you know it's all over. Final score: Bulls 87, Jazz 86.

You did it. You knew what you needed to do, and you did it. Because you belong out here on the court, and no matter if you retire this year, next year, in ten years, you always will.

There's no one else like you. Greatest of all time? You'll take it.

ANDREW WiGGiNS
HiGH FLYER

Andrew Wiggins can fly.

Well, maybe that's not exactly true, but he can soar through the air in a way that seems more like a superhero about to take flight than a normal human leaping to make a basket.

The Minnesota Timberwolves star makes it look easy. But all that great technique comes from lots and lots of practice. Each thrilling slam dunk he makes now builds on all the other dunks he's made along the way.

And there have been a lot.

There was his first-ever slam dunk, made when he was thirteen years old and living in Vaughan, Ontario. Anytime Andrew and his friends weren't at school, they were at the local recreation center playing basketball, so he had plenty of time to practice.

That original dunk may not have been anything fancy, but running up, springing to the basket, jamming the ball over the rim for the very first time ever—it was unforgettable.

He had another standout dunk not too long after, when he was in ninth grade. While playing a pickup game with his buddies, he saw an opening, and he went for it.

Picking up extra speed on his way to the basket like an airplane getting ready for takeoff, he catapulted himself up to the net. When he slammed the ball in—CRASH!—glass came raining down. He had shattered the backboard!

Andrew cringed as he reported the damage to the rec center workers, but they weren't mad—just amazed. They'd only ever seen that happen on TV.

His skills—and his dunks—kept getting better from there. He was always practicing, always training to make himself that much faster or more precise.

After Andrew moved to Kansas and became a star on his high school's basketball team, he competed in the McDonald's All-American slam dunk contest.

People still talk about Andrew's reverse-360 between-the-legs dunk. After he launched himself into the air, he spun in a complete circle away from the basket while looping the ball between his legs and then—*SLAM!*—hammering that ball through the net. The crowd went wild.

It was clear: Andrew was destined for the NBA, an even larger stage for him to show off his incredible abilities—including those dunks.

But after being the number one overall draft pick in 2014, he didn't have the smoothest start. Getting used to the size of the NBA, the speed, the talent, not to mention the nonstop schedule . . . it was hard at first.

It took Andrew until his sixth game to make one of his signature dunks. But once he did, he felt like a weight had been lifted. He could do this, even in the NBA. He was a great athlete finding his feet.

Since then, he's become a top player for
the Timberwolves. And he's kept up with
his amazing dunks, boasting one of the
best vertical jumps in the NBA at forty-
four inches. (That means he could jump
over the head of the average six-year-old!)

One memorable dunk came later in his rookie year against the Utah Jazz, where Andrew saw seven-foot-tall defender Rudy Gobert guarding the basket and thought, *I can do this.*

Using the floor as a springboard, he jumped into the air, reached up above Gobert's outstretched fingers, and dunked the ball. Worth watching in slo-mo, and part of the reason he earned his Rookie of the Year title.

54

Another famous dunk came against the Miami Heat in October 2017. It was the fourth quarter, with only a few minutes left, and the Heat's Josh Richardson was keeping in step beside him.

But Andrew roared forward, and a few feet from the basket, he took off. Once he was airborne, the defender was helpless—Andrew sailed to the net and nailed that dunk like a king.

Of course, Andrew Wiggins has a lot of other skills in his arsenal—he's a great scorer, good defender, and all-around solid teammate—but his secret weapon is those fantastic dunks.

And the best part is, Andrew has never forgotten his early days in Vaughan, where it all started. In 2016, he returned to his childhood rec center and donated some new equipment—including new backboards. And he marked the backboard he had once shattered as a kid with a handprint in blue paint.

It was his thank-you to the place where he'd honed his skills. And a way of saying to the next generation: Andrew Wiggins dunked here. Maybe you can too.

KING JAMES MAKES HISTORY

It's Game 7 of the NBA Finals, fourth quarter, the score is tied, and I can't sit still.

Dad can't either, so he gets up to grab more snacks.

The Golden State Warriors are going to beat the Cleveland Cavaliers, exactly like they did last year. I just know it.

I can't even believe the Cavs pulled themselves back up after being down three games to one. But no team has ever won a championship coming from that far behind.

"Listen, I'm the world's biggest Cavs fan, but they're not going to win," I say to my sister, Sam.

She shakes her head. "To start with, *I'm* the bigger fan. I liked them first." Sam always says that. It's only because she's two years older than me. "And second— LeBron's going to win this. He promised," she adds.

I roll my eyes. "Come on. The Cavs have never won a championship. Ever. It's not like LeBron's a miracle worker."

Maybe I'm still mad at him for leaving the Cavaliers, even if it was just for four years. I mean, Cleveland drafted him right out of high school. They had first pick and they chose him!

So what if they weren't the strongest? LeBron James grew up in northeast Ohio, so Cleveland was like his hometown team. He belonged here.

But then seven years in, he left to play with the Miami Heat. He broke people's hearts.

"If he hadn't gone to Miami, he wouldn't be as good as he is today," Sam says for the millionth time.

"Yeah, right." I chew on a fingernail. "Oh!" LeBron just missed a basket. Still tied.

Sam keeps talking. "He needed to win a couple of championships with the Heat."

"And lose a couple," I add.

"*And* lose a couple," Sam repeats. "You remember what happened after the Heat lost the 2011 NBA Finals? LeBron worked even harder. He trained with Hakeem Olajuwon. Hakeem the Dream!"

though he was pretty much the best, LeBron wanted to be even better.

"He worked hard and changed his whole game. He started shooting closer to the basket, overpowering the defense . . ."

Dad comes back in with an overflowing chip bowl. "What'd I miss?" He plops down on the couch.

"Still tied," Sam says.

"LeBron never should have left Cleveland. Right, Dad?" I say.

"Oooh!" Sam yells. LeBron just got fouled by Steph Curry, and they're both on the ground.

Dad winces. "Well," he says. "Maybe he had to leave to realize how much Cleveland really meant to him. And now that he's back, he wants to win this more than ever. To bring the trophy home."

I nod and feel a bit of hope sparkle in my chest.

There's only two minutes left in the game, and everyone stops talking. I sit with my hands clamped together. Sam jiggles her leg. Dad eats chips.

"No one's scoring," Sam says, shaking her head. Each team is trying, but no one can get the ball in. They're clearly tired.

"Whoever gets this next basket is going to win the game," Dad says, and we all know it's true.

One of my favorite Cavs players,
Kyrie Irving, shoots but misses, and the
Warriors get the rebound.

"Nooo!" I yell. Andre Iguodala is
barreling down the court. He passes to
Curry, Curry to Iguodala, who's about
to score . . . "It's in, it's in, it's in—"

But it's *not* in.

"WHOOAAA," we all yell, because LeBron James BLOCKED THE SHOT!

And it wasn't just a simple block. He came from way back, crossed the court like lightning, and flew over in front of the net, where he caught the ball against the backboard before it went in.

It looked impossible, but somehow he'd made the save. We're on our feet, watching the replay.

"How did he do that?!" I say to Sam, but she's just yelling, "Woooo!"

It's unbelievable. Now the Cavaliers have a time-out and we're still sitting here, amazed by what we just saw. And I'm thinking, *We're going to win this.*

Time-out's done, and it's clear LeBron's save did exactly what he'd wanted it to. It gave the Cavs the edge.

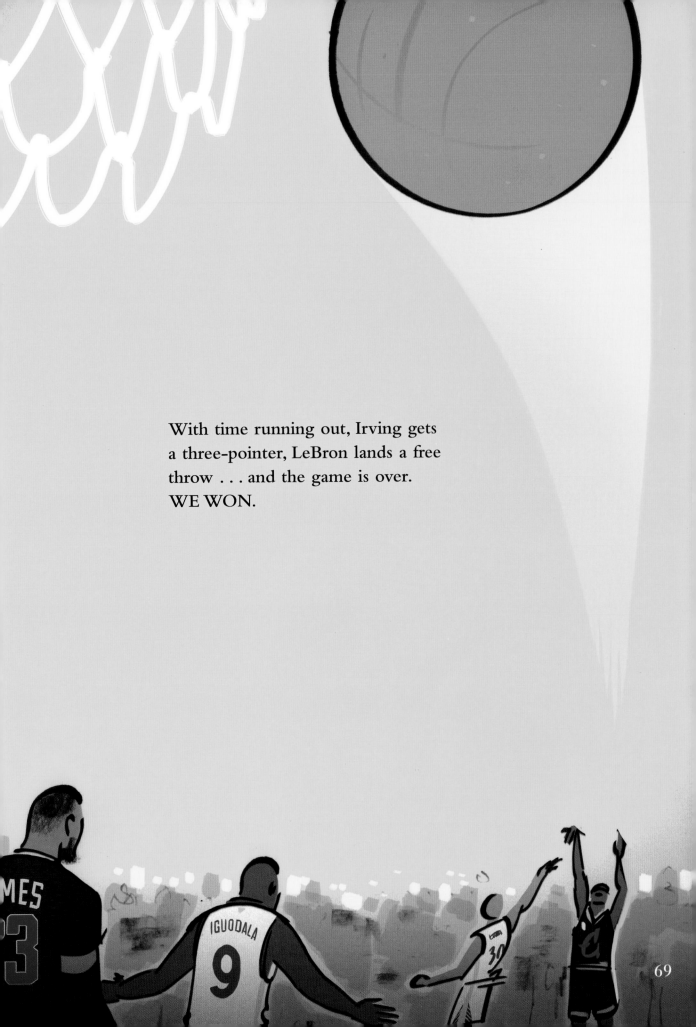

With time running out, Irving gets
a three-pointer, LeBron lands a free
throw . . . and the game is over.
WE WON.

The Cavaliers won the championship. For the first time ever in the history of the NBA.

LeBron is crying, he's so happy. I might be crying too.

"Told you King James would come through," Sam says.

And I can't argue with her. Not one bit.

THE WORLD'S BIGGEST BASKETBALL LESSON

The gym was full of hundreds of excited kids, all waiting for the NBA basketball star.

He had come all the way to New Delhi, India, to take them—and thousands more kids watching on video screens across the country—through some drills.

They were hoping to set a world record for the biggest basketball lesson ever.

71

Breaking a record would be pretty great.
But even greater? Being able to learn
basketball skills from one of their heroes.

Finally, he walked onto the stage.
2017 NBA champion and Finals MVP,
eight-time all-star, youngest player ever
to win a scoring title, Kevin Durant.

And there he stood: a tall, skinny
eight-year-old boy.

Okay, Kevin wasn't that eight-year-old anymore. He was grown up now, a world-class athlete, getting paid millions.

But standing in front of the crowd, he felt like that little boy again. Because he'd been just like these kids: eager, nervous, ready to learn.

And boy, had he needed basketball.

When Kevin was a little kid growing up in Seat Pleasant, Maryland, he hadn't really fit in. Quiet and shy, he wasn't big on getting noticed . . . but his height made him stick out no matter what he did.

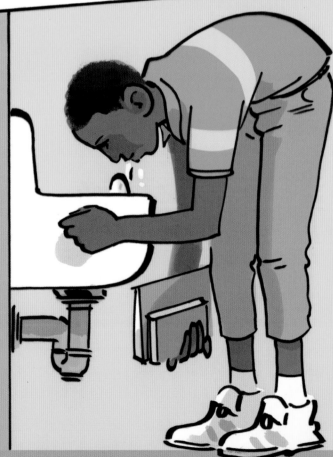

He was taller than all the other children in his class. So much taller that his mother would ask his teachers to put him at the ends of lineups so he wouldn't stand out quite so much.

Still, the other kids made fun of him, and he knew he looked different. It bothered Kevin. A lot.

Luckily, his mother had a plan. She started sending him and his older brother, Tony, to the local recreation center. She figured there, Kevin could keep busy, find friends, and play some sports. She figured there, he'd find his place.

And she was right.

On that very first day, Kevin took a basketball lesson from a coach named Taras Brown, who everybody just called Stink. And right from the start, Kevin took to the game.

He liked the feel of the ball in his hands, the squeak of his sneakers on the court floor . . . plus, in basketball, being tall was actually a good thing.

Kevin was lucky to have three coaches when he started who really made him the player he would become.

Stink helped teach Kevin all the skills he'd need—running, dribbling, layups, footwork. And he helped Kevin get stronger and tougher.

After the indoor drills, Stink would take Kevin outside to run a steep hill near the center. Up and down, up and down, over and over, until Kevin's legs felt like jelly.

His second great teacher was a man named Charles Craig—the kids called him Big Chucky. He coached the rec center's basketball team for nine-year-olds, but he could tell Kevin had potential. So he gave him a spot on the team, even though he was a whole year younger than the other kids.

Out on the court, Kevin started learning how to work with teammates and set up plays. He began to understand the rhythm of the game.

But maybe the most important coach of all was his mother. She would go watch his training and cheer him on. But also, she would never let him slack off. Even if Kevin had done all the layups that Stink asked for and was panting for breath, she would look at him and say, "How about ten more?"

When he wasn't on the court, his mom would remind him to keep training—to do his sit-ups and push-ups, or maybe go play some pickup ball down the street.

She was always driving him to push himself because she knew it took hard work to be good at something. And she believed he was special.

In his spare time, Kevin would watch basketball and study the plays, dreaming of one day being on the Toronto Raptors like his idol, Vince Carter.

But as much as he loved the game, as Kevin got older there were times when he'd wanted to quit. It was hard to lose games, or to miss the big shot and let his teammates down. He wasn't always sure he was good enough.

So his mother would
say, "Just finish out the
season. See how you
feel then." In the end,
he always stayed with it.
    And now here he
was, looking out at
this sea of faces. Taking
these kids through some
ball-handling and foot-
work exercises, just like
he'd done when he was
little.

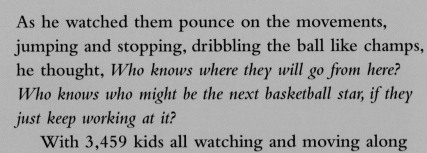

As he watched them pounce on the movements, jumping and stopping, dribbling the ball like champs, he thought, *Who knows where they will go from here? Who knows who might be the next basketball star, if they just keep working at it?*

With 3,459 kids all watching and moving along with him, Kevin had to smile. Everyone was working together, sweating hard, and having fun. This was what the game was all about, for sure.

KD had definitely found his place in basketball. And he hoped some of these kids would too.

Naismith
BALL

It was the middle of winter at the college in Springfield, Massachusetts, and something had to be done.

The boys—well, they were young men, really—were rowdy as could be. They were pushing and shoving in the halls, fidgeting during classes, even throwing food at lunch. It was too cold outside to run around, and they were cooped up and stir-crazy.

The teachers were fed up. So James Naismith,
a gym teacher who worked at the school, was given
a task: Come up with a new indoor game that can
tire these students out. Please!

He was given just two weeks.

At first, James tried keeping it simple.
The boys liked a good game of soccer—
couldn't that just be moved inside?

No, that didn't work. There just
wasn't enough space. The students were
booting the ball clear across the room,
bouncing it off the walls. It was chaos.

They loved lacrosse too—maybe that would work instead?

No, it was a disaster. They were just too wild to play the game in such close quarters. People wound up getting smacked with sticks, and James himself was nearly beaned by a lacrosse ball.

As the days went on, he started to lose hope. How was he supposed to come up with something new? All the best games had already been invented.

Maybe the boys would just overrun the school, he would quit, and that would be that.

Or maybe . . . maybe he just needed to think beyond organized sport. Back when he was a kid living in farm country in Almonte, Ontario, he played all sorts of games with his friends just to pass the time. The one he'd liked most was called "duck on a rock."

You'd put a rock on top of a tree stump or boulder. One person had to be the guard and stand off to the side. Then everyone else would take turns throwing stones at the rock to knock it off its perch.

If you missed, you had to try to get your stone back before the guard tagged you. James and his friends used to play for hours.

What about a game like that, he thought, where someone guarded a target and you had to hit it. But instead of using rocks, what about a ball? And the target could be . . . yes, a peach basket!

James nailed baskets high on the walls at each end of the gym to act as goals.

But there was one problem: getting the ball back out. He set up a stepladder beside each basket, so someone could just climb up there anytime the ball went in and fetch it. Easy enough!

He came up with a few basic rules, and the next day, he let his students play.

That first game didn't go so well. Players were holding onto the ball and running with it, which meant everyone grabbing and shoving to try to get their turn. Eventually, there was just one big tangle of boys in the middle of the gym, scuffling. What a mess.

James didn't give up, though.

He just added some new rules.

A player couldn't hold the ball and run with it; he'd have to pass it to move it down the court. Pushing and hitting and tripping weren't allowed. Any horseplay like that would result in a foul.

In the end, he had thirteen rules in all, which he posted outside the gym the next day.

"Oh, we're trying this again, are we?" one of his students said, reading the rules on his way to gym class. "Basket ball, he calls it." All the boys laughed. But they gave it another try.

This time, the game went better. Even though the students found throwing a soccer ball instead of kicking it a little odd at first, and it was a bit slow having to go up a ladder every time someone got a basket, it was also fun.

Really fun.

They started asking to play it all the time, even when it was warm enough to go outside again. They told all their friends about this new game and taught them the rules.

Soon enough, it began catching on all across the country. Girls played too!

As it got more popular, little changes were made here and there. Players started using a new bouncier type of ball and dribbling it while they moved. And the peach baskets? They were replaced with wire rims and, later, nets. (No more stepladders!)

But at its heart, it was—and still is—the same game first played on that snowy December day in 1891.

For his part, James never quite understood why the game was so popular. Even though he'd created it, basketball wasn't his favorite sport. He preferred wrestling and gymnastics.

Still, there was something about basketball.
From the lowliest one-on-one match
on an outdoor court to the championship
NBA game in a packed stadium, it brought
people together. Just as it had brought
together that group of bored young
men in the dead of winter.

James may not have truly understood his own genius, but he had to
admit one thing: Basketball was
here to stay.

Welcome, shoes and boots, to the long-overdue opening of the Basketball Shoe Hall of Fame! We all know that without us, the players wouldn't be able to run as fast or jump as high—or look as good doing it. So without further ado, I present our first inductees!

CHUCK TAYLOR ALL-STAR (1917)

These shoes are the originals! When they first came out, they were called Non-Skids, but luckily a few years later, Converse sponsored a basketball team called the All Stars . . . that included a player named Chuck Taylor.

Chuck traveled around the United States
teaching basketball and spreading the word
about these amazing sneakers—and he also
helped Converse improve the shoe's design.
In the end, they named them after him:
Chuck Taylor All-Stars.

They're iconic, they're classic . . .
and they look basically the same even
a hundred years later! Not so bad for
antiques!

ADIDAS JABBAR (1971)

Today, most top basketball players have their own line of shoes, but it wasn't always this way. In 1971, adidas did it first, when they made a shoe for basketball great Kareem Abdul-Jabbar. They worked with him to make something that he could wear proudly and that his fans could too.

For this landmark creation, adidas used their famous design (with the three lines along the side) but added a special touch: a sketch of Abdul-Jabbar's smiling face on the tongue. People went nuts for it, and we have this shoe—and Kareem—to thank for all the signature shoes ever since.

NIKE AIR FORCE 1 (1982)

Funnily enough, a lot of shoes up to this point weren't that supportive to the foot. It was hard trying to invent something that would stand up to wear and tear but also be cushioning. Nike Air Force 1s had it all.

NBA players loved their combination of snazzy and sturdy. And so did everyone else. Nike almost stopped making them two years in, but luckily they realized their mistake—and the Air Force 1 has since become the biggest-selling athletic shoe in history.

AIR JORDAN 1 (1985)

Michael Jordan didn't just wow people with his unmatched talent on the court. He also rocked the sneaker world when he teamed up with Nike for the Air Jordan 1. This guy was the best of the best, and the shoes were too.

Famously, the NBA banned the black-and-red pair from games, saying players had to wear shoes that were mostly white. Of course, MJ wore them anyway, and the dispute made the shoes so famous, everyone wanted a pair. They're still probably the best-known basketball sneakers to this day.

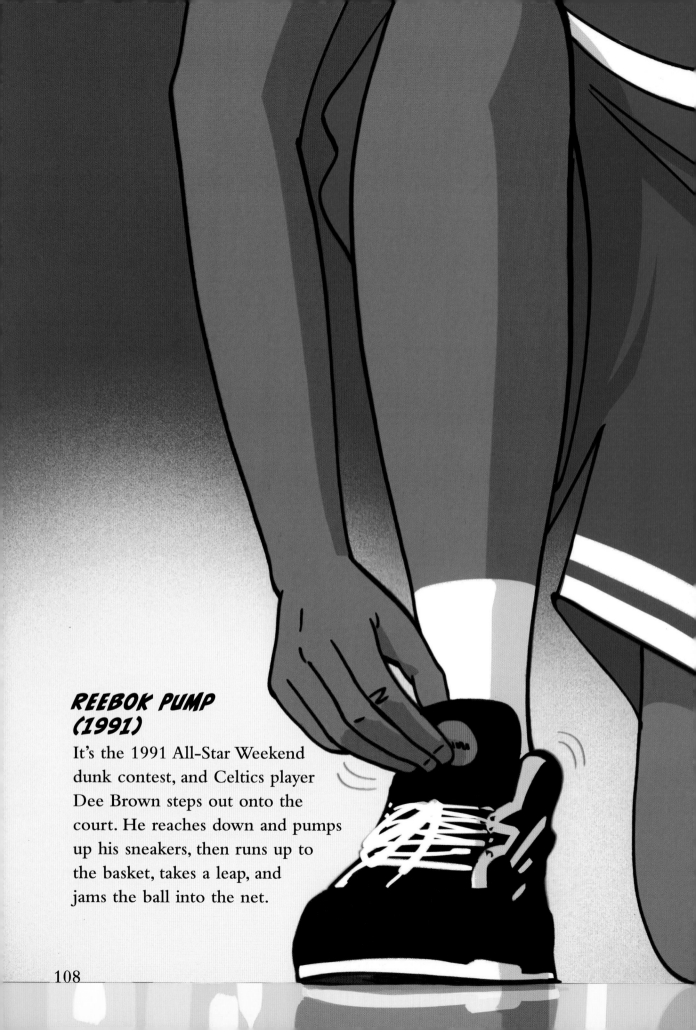

REEBOK PUMP (1991)

It's the 1991 All-Star Weekend dunk contest, and Celtics player Dee Brown steps out onto the court. He reaches down and pumps up his sneakers, then runs up to the basket, takes a leap, and jams the ball into the net.

Was it the shoes? Maybe. Reebok had come out with a new pair of sneakers with air pockets that you could inflate yourself—by pressing the pump on the tongue of the shoe. Everyone wanted their own pair, to pump up their game . . . and maybe pull off a slam dunk too.

NIKE AIR SWOOPES (1996)

Sheryl Swoopes and the American women's basketball team won every single one of their games at the 1996 Olympics and showed the world what women's basketball could be. She was the first player chosen for the WNBA when it started up that same year. A four-time WNBA champion, she is probably the best player the league has ever seen.

So it makes sense that Sheryl Swoopes had the very first women's signature basketball shoe—the Nike Air Swoopes. The shoe was modern, strong, iconic . . . and a huge step forward for female athletes. Thanks, Sheryl.

NIKE LEBRON 15 (2017)

These shoes are top of the line, high-powered, and stylish . . . just like LeBron himself. Since they are made out of Nike's BattleKnit, they are super flexible but also heavy-duty and supportive, so they can handle the hard landings from LeBron's famous dunks. (All that jumping is hard on the knees!)

Nike worked all the best features of LeBron's line of shoes into the LeBron 15, leading some people to call the shoe the best of its generation . . . just like LeBron himself!

112

FINDING A NEW HOME TEAM

Swoosh. Two points! I'm killing time, practicing my free throws in the gym. If I go home, I'll just have to do more packing.

Out of the corner of my eye, I see Coach Sharma heading over. "You've been shooting hoops for a while," she says, coming to stand by the basket. "You worried about the big move?"

I glance at her and nod. My family's moving to Houston, Texas.

A whole other state.

"Have you ever heard of Yao Ming?" she asks. It seems like it's out of the blue, but I know Coach. She likes to talk basketball, but she's always got a lesson hidden somewhere.

"Yeah," I say. "All I remember is he's super tall." I take a shot. The ball bounces off the rim.

Coach grabs it and chucks it back to me. "Seven foot six. One of the tallest NBA players ever. He was on the Houston Rockets. Your new home team."

I trace the lines on the
ball with my finger. I don't
think Houston will ever
feel like home.

"Yao Ming grew up in Shanghai. Before he came here, he was a star in the Chinese Basketball Association. Then he got chosen by the Rockets and became the first-ever international player to be a number one overall draft pick. And only the second Chinese-born player in NBA history."

"Pretty amazing," I say.

Coach really knows her stuff.

YAO MING 11

"But," she says, "that meant Yao had to move from his home to a whole new country, learn a whole new language, and play ball with a whole new bunch of people. As talented as he was, there were so many expectations on him, not just from NBA fans but from his millions of fans in China too."

Millions. Yikes. I turn back to the basket, imagining all those people are watching me. I aim, shoot . . . and miss.

Coach passes the ball back. "It was a big change for Yao because things in America were so different. Including basketball. In the Chinese league, other players would often back off because he was so big and strong. In the NBA, the game was rougher, and people would take him on no matter how tall he was. So there was a lot to learn."

"There always is, someplace new," I mumble, repeating something my mom told me.

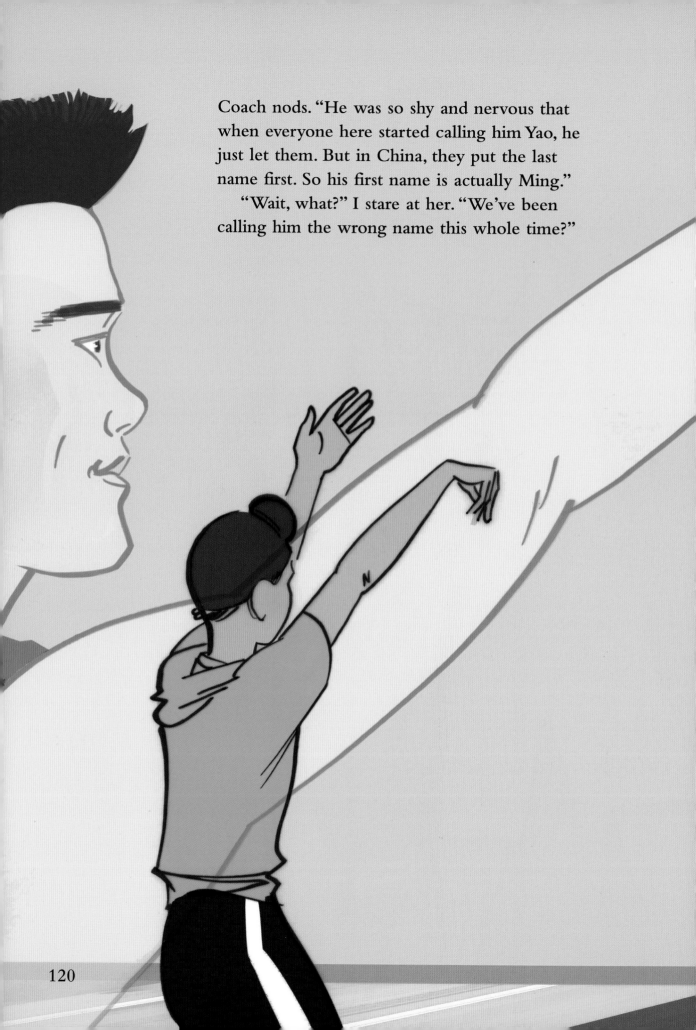

Coach nods. "He was so shy and nervous that when everyone here started calling him Yao, he just let them. But in China, they put the last name first. So his first name is actually Ming."

"Wait, what?" I stare at her. "We've been calling him the wrong name this whole time?"

120

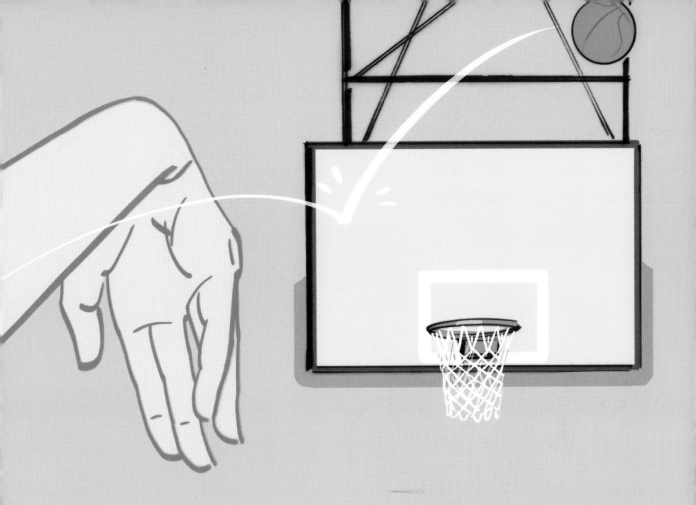

"Yup," she says with a shrug. "But that was the least of his problems. He only got to Houston ten days before his rookie season started, so he hardly had any training time with his team. Suddenly, there he was, out on the court with all those fans watching. In his first game, he didn't score a single point."

I shoot . . . Too high. It bounces off the backboard.

"But you know, practice makes perfect," Coach says with a smile. "He just kept on working at it. And soon, he was scoring with the best of them. His career average was nineteen points per game."

Nineteen points. That's more than our whole team scores most games.

"And get this—in his first time playing against Shaquille O'Neal and the Lakers, he blocked Shaq's shots three times in a row! He was truly one of the best centers of his time. Yao became an eight-time NBA All-Star, and in 2009, he took the Rockets to the second round of the playoffs for the first time in more than ten years.

"Plus, he gave a huge boost to basketball in China and inspired millions of kids there—and here too!—to give the game a try."

123

I pretend I'm Yao and stand up as
straight as I can, take aim, and try to
think like I'm seven feet tall. Ready,
aim, easy does it . . . I make the bucket!
"Nice!" Coach says.

I grin. "So, are you saying I should sprout three feet and become the star on my new school's team, just like Yao?"

She laughs. "Yeah, sure," she says. "Or maybe if you get on the team, take your time, and play your best, that new school won't be so bad after all."

I think about it. "I'll try," I say. "Thanks, Coach."
I toss her the ball. "I guess I should be getting
home—I've got a lot of packing to do."

7 SECONDS OR LESS

There was Steve Nash, out on the floor, dribbling down the court like he was the only one on it.

When he had the ball, you could count on something amazing happening, you just didn't know what. And that was why it worked. The other team had no idea what was coming.

Maybe it was all that time he'd spent playing soccer as a kid in Victoria, British Columbia, but he had something unique— an inventiveness—that made him tough to pin down.

And so he made it look easy: busting through the defense, into the paint, scoring two points. All in a matter of seconds. That was Steve— bringing home another win for the Phoenix Suns.

Steve hadn't always been with the Suns. They had drafted him when he was starting out, but then he'd been traded to the Dallas Mavericks. That was where his talent had really started to shine.

But when he turned thirty, the Mavericks decided to let him go. They thought he wasn't worth keeping on, that he was getting old and slowing down.

Steve had something else in mind. He planned on speeding up. So he made a bold move and went back to Phoenix.

Fans were shocked: a top player like Nash, switching from the stellar Mavericks to a team that had just finished one of its worst seasons ever? It seemed like a huge risk.

But Steve knew what he was doing. The new Suns coach, Mike D'Antoni, wanted to rebuild the team. He wanted Steve to be the leader, the pacesetter. And the pace Mike had in mind? It was fast. Super fast.

In the NBA, the shot clock gives a team twenty-four seconds to try to score a basket. Mike wanted it done in seven. Down the court, ball to the net. *SWOOSH*. Seven seconds or less. For Steve? That was just his speed.

Around that time, lots of teams were focusing on defense, which meant slower games. Lower scores. Not as much action.

So when the new Phoenix Suns hit the court, people were dazzled. They were so speedy, so powerful, so exciting. All thanks to Steve Nash.

The other teams didn't know what hit them. Their usual tactics of blocking the basket with their biggest guys didn't seem to work with Steve. He would sneak right through them, unafraid of getting boxed in. He knew he'd get that ball where it needed to go.

Or he would mosey along, explode forward with a burst of speed, then pull up short, so the other guys couldn't stay on him. He'd find a pocket of space, take aim, and get a three-pointer.

And as for passing? He could thread the basketball through the tiniest of openings to a free teammate's hands. It felt like he could make the ball go right through people to its target.

Or he'd use an incredible fake-out move, where he'd rush forward as if going for a layup but then, without a backward glance, toss the ball behind him to one of his buddies. The defense would be stunned . . . while the Suns would get another two points.

Steve had a natural grace, a dancer's sense of how everyone was moving around him. Like a piece in a constantly moving puzzle, he could always find his place. And he could get the ball to anyone.

Even though he was a top shooter, that was what Steve liked best. Passing the ball so his teammates could show their stuff. The team was like family to him, and they knew it. So they played their very best.

By the end of the season, Steve had
turned the Suns completely around.
They'd gone from tanking to winning
more than sixty games. They even made
it to the Western Conference finals—
clobbering his old team, the Mavericks,
along the way.

Steve was named MVP, but he had so much more to be proud of.

He'd helped breathe new life into the Suns. He'd shown he was one of the best point guards in history. And he'd brought the fun back to basketball—seven seconds at a time.

THE REAL DEAL

The Phoenix Suns are ahead of the San Antonio Spurs by just a single point, and the kids sitting in the front row are watching closely. Nash takes a shot but the ball rebounds. Shaquille O'Neal wheels around and goes running after it. Full tilt. Right toward the stands.

Everyone's watching him hurtle closer and closer to the kids, thinking, *Oh, no. This can't be good.*

But just in time, he leaps—right over top of them, into the third row. The kids are saved, no one is hurt, and the crowd just got an amazing show.

Shaq climbs back out, dusts himself off, and gets back to the game.

Shaq fans everywhere love this moment, because it says a lot about him: He always gave his all, he put on a great show, he cared about his fans . . . and he's such a big guy that once he got going, it could be hard for him to stop.

143

To start with, Shaq is physically large—seven foot one and 325 pounds. So on all of his teams he was always the "big man"—a basketball term for the tallest and strongest player, usually the center, who plays close to the basket.

144

Shaq is also larger than life. His personality and sense of humor are well known, even to people who don't like basketball. And sometimes it can seem like he's, well, everywhere.

145

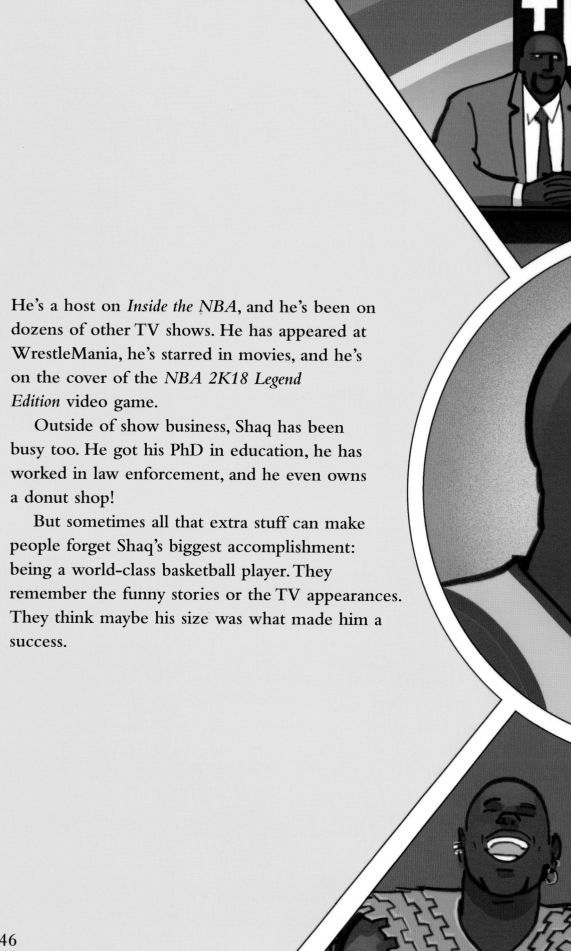

He's a host on *Inside the NBA*, and he's been on dozens of other TV shows. He has appeared at WrestleMania, he's starred in movies, and he's on the cover of the *NBA 2K18 Legend Edition* video game.

Outside of show business, Shaq has been busy too. He got his PhD in education, he has worked in law enforcement, and he even owns a donut shop!

But sometimes all that extra stuff can make people forget Shaq's biggest accomplishment: being a world-class basketball player. They remember the funny stories or the TV appearances. They think maybe his size was what made him a success.

147

Sure, being so big was part of who
Shaq was on the court. He could
make some wicked plays by plowing
right through the opposing team to
the basket. He was powerful. And
boy, could he jump.

But for a big guy, he could be super fast, and he had finesse too. It was the perfect combo. And never did he show off these skills better than during his years with the Los Angeles Lakers.

Take his buzzer beater against the Utah Jazz in April 1997. Right beforehand, he told the coach he was going to save the game. And he did—with a fadeaway jump shot just as the clock ticked to zero. So smooth.

HOME

GUEST

Or the game on March 6, 2000—Shaq's twenty-eighth birthday—when the Lakers were playing the L.A. Clippers, and Shaq scored a career-high sixty-one points. Afterward, even the Clippers' coach said nothing could have been done. Shaq was unstoppable.

But he wasn't just great on offense. His blocks were legendary. Like the one against Miami Heat player Tim Hardaway, who was heading in fast for a layup . . . when Shaq came out of nowhere and slapped the ball right out of his hand. Tim wound up on the floor, thinking, *What just happened?*

Maybe one of Shaq's very best moments, though, was the clutch play in Game 7 of the Western Conference finals in 2000. Up against the Portland Trail Blazers, the Lakers came from behind in the fourth quarter to tie the score.

With a few seconds left on the clock, Kobe Bryant sent Shaq the alley-oop pass and Shaq met the ball in the air miles above the basket, slamming it through the hoop. This electrifying win broke a dry spell for the Lakers and propelled them on to the NBA Finals. There, they won their first championship title in over ten years. Shaq would lead the Lakers to two more NBA Finals victories in a row, but this first one was the sweetest.

And Shaq wasn't done after his Lakers years. He went on to win *another* championship with the Miami Heat in 2006. No matter what else he's achieved, it's pretty clear: Shaq was one of basketball's greats.

So it's no wonder that even back in 1993, when he was in his rookie year with the Orlando Magic, Shaq was already making headlines.

The team was in New Jersey, playing against the Nets, and Shaq saw the chance for a dunk. He leaped up, jammed the ball through the hoop, hung on the rim . . . and brought the entire basket down. Backboard. Net. Metal supports. THE WHOLE THING.

Luckily everyone was okay . . . except the basket. And as for Shaq? It was just the start of a long list of "best of" moments that are as unforgettable and outsized as the man himself.

CANDACE PARKER CHAMPION

Basketball was always a part of Candace Parker's life. Her father was in the NBA, and her two older brothers played the game too. She started going to games when she was just a baby, and she never stopped.

To her, basketball was like another member of the family. An annoying younger sibling that was always trying to get her attention.

155

Sure, Candace liked basketball. But she didn't think she'd ever be as good as her father or brothers.

So she got into soccer instead, dreaming of one day making it to the Olympics.

But as she got older and taller, her father wondered if maybe basketball still had a chance.

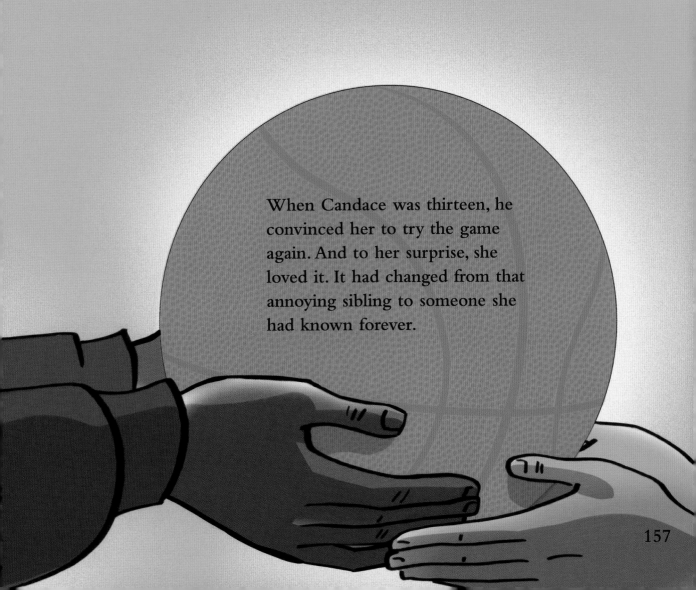

When Candace was thirteen, he convinced her to try the game again. And to her surprise, she loved it. It had changed from that annoying sibling to someone she had known forever.

Even though she'd started late, all her knowledge of the game made basketball a natural fit. And her soccer skills came in handy too.

On her high school team, Candace made her family proud. At the age of fifteen, she slam dunked for the first time.

The dunking didn't stop there—a few years later, she won the McDonald's All-American slam dunk contest, over all the boys who competed. And you can bet the college coaches were watching.

Coach Pat Summitt, in particular, saw Candace's brilliance and nabbed her for the University of Tennessee. She and Candace clicked, and Candace's skills grew more and more astounding with Pat as her guide. The team won back-to-back championships.

Soon after, in 2008, Candace took the leap to the WNBA and was the first overall draft pick, chosen by the Los Angeles Sparks.

She'd made it. Just like her brother Anthony and her father, Candace was a professional basketball player.

Basketball had become her best friend. She couldn't imagine ever living without it.

In her first year with the Sparks, Candace won Rookie of the Year and MVP in the same season, something very few basketball players have ever done.

That same year, she got on to the U.S. Olympic team and brought home a gold medal. Another dream achieved.

As time went on, Candace became an all-star player, was top ten in the league for skills from scoring to rebounds to assists, and won gold at another Olympics.

But there was one more dream she wanted more than anything. To win a championship. Because it would prove that everything she'd worked for had been worth it.

Year after year, the Los Angeles Sparks would make it to the semifinals, or even the finals, but they could never seem to clinch the title.

Basketball was starting to feel a bit like that annoying sibling again. Teasing Candace by holding this one thing she really wanted just out of reach.

Then came 2016, which got off to a rough start. First, she found out she hadn't been picked for the Olympic team. Then, and so much worse, her coach and friend Pat Summitt passed away.

No one would have blamed Candace for not playing as well that season, with so much on her mind.

But somehow she stayed strong, even with a heavy heart, and she took her team all the way to the finals.

It came down to Game 5 against the Minnesota Lynx, the top-ranked team in the league. Whoever won would get the trophy.

There in Minnesota, surrounded by thousands of fans cheering for the other team, Candace made up her mind: This was it. This was her championship.

She gave everything to that game. And she was a force, scoring 28 points and getting a ton of rebounds. And when the buzzer sounded . . . the Sparks had won. Candace had won.

She'd achieved her dream—for herself,
for her team, for Coach Summitt.
    And for basketball. The game was
her rock, her soulmate.

She hoped she'd done it proud.